In Praise
of Fertile Land

In Praise
of Fertile Land

An anthology of poetry, parable, and story

Edited by Claudia Mauro

Whit
Press

Hugo House, 1634 Eleventh Avenue, Seattle, WA 98122, whitpress@aol.com

In Praise of Fertile Land
Edited by Claudia Mauro
Design by Tracy Lamb

Published by
Whit Press, Inc.
Richard Hugo House
1634 Eleventh Avenue
Seattle, WA 98122
whitpress@aol.com

•

ISBN 0-9720205-1-9

Library of Congress Control Number
2003108242

Acknowledgments

Whit Press gratefully acknowledges the generous support of the following organizations. This book was made possible by:

The Breneman-Jaech Foundation

The King County Office of Arts and Cultural Affairs

cultural **arts** heritage historic preservation public art
development authority of king county

The Seattle Foundation

Much of the research and editorial work for this project was completed during residencies at **The Helen Riaboff Whiteley Center** at the University of Washington, Friday Harbor Laboratories, and **Hedgebrook Women Writer's Retreat** on Whidbey Island, Washington. Whit Press is also deeply grateful for the support, vision, and commitment to this project from the following individuals: Nancy Nordoff, Moira and Ken Mumma, and Marcia and Mohammed Daoudi.

Special thanks to educator Dr. Shelley Tucker and the terrific poets of her 2nd, 3rd, and 4th grade classes at McGilvra Elementary School in Seattle who adopted this project wholeheartedly and contributed many excellent poems; Jody Aliesan for her keen eye, unwavering integrity and commitment to farmland, and the belief in poetry as an elemental force for change; Tracy Lamb for yet another magnificent book design; Felicia Gonzalez for invaluable help with project design, fundraising, and editorial suggestions; thanks to Nassim Assefi, Carol Estes, Joan Fiset, Gitana Garofalo, Jeb Lewis, John Mifsud, and Katie Kay; and to all the writers and publishers who donated their work to this book.

For you all, my most heartfelt thanks and gratitude.

To my grandmother,
Margherita Nobile Chiuchiolo,
1897-1992,
for the life of my heart.

Heaven met earth at her kitchen table.

M ost of the surface of our planet is seawater, ice, rock, desert, and forest. A very small proportion can support the growing of food. *In Praise of Fertile Land* educates, inspires, and spurs us to protect these lands and their stewards for the sake of our survival.

In the United States, our local food-producing land is threatened by development. Fully 86 percent of our fruits and vegetables and 63 percent of our dairy products are produced on the edge of urban areas. The United States is losing two acres of farmland every minute. We're losing the most fertile and productive land most quickly. The problem is wasteful land use. The villain is sprawl.

There's a second threat to local food security. For more than fifty years a handful of agriculture conglomerates, assisted by federal farm policy, has been working to drive small farmers off their land by paying them less for their produce than it costs to grow it. The result: forced loans from the conglomerate's banks, the burden of mortgages, the dispossession of foreclosures, and the sale of land to corporate-controlled agribusiness.

Two thirds of all farmers—including vegetable, fruit, and dairy farmers—receive no direct financial farm support. Most government subsidies go to the same few corporate agribusinesses: ten percent of landowners in ten states ordering fence-to-fence plantings of commodity crops such as cotton, rice, wheat, corn, and soybeans as part of "futures" speculation in international export markets. These corporations hire managers who don't live on the land.

When global gambling in export futures causes crop surpluses and low prices, effects rip through the agricultural economy and small farmers lose their livelihood. With them go rural communities and our local food security. The false justification that small farms are "inefficient" adds insult to injury.

Studies have shown that small organic and sustainable farms are more productive, more efficient, and contribute to local economies. Their farmers are better stewards of natural resources. In addition to producing food free of poisons, their practices build living soil, shelter wildlife, conserve energy, and protect the quality of air and water. Small farm use of capital, land, and labor is more integrated and socially just.

You can help. Buy locally produced food from as close to the source as you can—with community-supported agriculture (CSA) farm shares, at farmers' markets, or from retailers who purchase from local farmers. Buy copies of this book for your friends and family. Make a contribution to the Farmland Fund.

The Farmland Fund is grateful to Whit Press for the publication of *In Praise of Fertile Land* and for the gift of its royalties. Their support and yours helps make it possible to secure and preserve threatened farmland in Washington State and keep it in organic production—for the sake of farming and farming livelihood, local, fresh organic produce, and loyalty between people who grow the food and people who eat it.

Jody Aliesan
President, PCC Farmland Fund

4201 Roosevelt Way NE
Seattle, WA 98105
206.547.1222 tel
206.545.7131 fax
farmlandfund@pccsea.com
www.pccnaturalmarkets.com/farmlandfund/

Introduction

Growing up on the edge of New York City, I heard the old joke that "city kids thought milk came from bottles." To the west of my Long Island town lay one of the world's densest metropolitan areas, to the east stretched family farms and open country.

Forty years later, those farms are mostly gone and suburban sprawl has blurred the distinction between urban and rural—a pattern repeated throughout the country.

Now our hectic, increasingly urban lives perpetuate the convincing illusion that we are all independent from the land and labor that provides our food. More and more we live and choose as if sustenance were simply a matter of access to enough money and a nearby grocery conglomerate.

But the loss of arable land to development costs us more than economic models reflect. When we lose farmland, we lose our sense of connection to the cycles and seasons of the earth, and to the people who grow and harvest our food. We have come to count on our "milk coming from cartons."

On the other hand, poems written and read and stories told and retold are acts of interdependence—community action. In the words of poet Czeslaw Milosz " *The purpose of poetry is to remind us how difficult it is to remain just one person.* "

In Praise of Fertile Land is a unique nonprofit publishing project. It was created as a tool for protecting and preserving our remaining farmlands. All the royalties from the sale of this book (and in many cases the entire purchase price) go directly to programs and organizations that preserve farmland.

Included here are the poems and stories of our neighbors, our kids, and our finest poets and storytellers. These are poems for the kitchen table—stories to be read to each other aloud, talked about, savored. Dig in!

Claudia Mauro, Editor

People of the Earth — 15

Contents

At the Table ·   101

For the Love of Earth   125

Contents

People of the Earth

Good house—
sparrows out back
feasting in the millet.

—*Bashō*
1644-1694

You Make the Earth Good by Your Work

Remedio was leaning on his shovel, looking out over the desert, talking to me as if he were *listening* for the things he wanted to say, for the meaning to rise out of the desert and come to him.

"I have been thinking about this many nights now, about when I leave here and go, no more on this earth, that I should begin to prepare for that. And that's why I'm working today, to make a new field and a shrine nearby. See, my mind has been going this way, that I should be planting things. Leaving little green things growing up, and gathering beautiful rocks from the desert for a shrine to the saint who has taken care of me. That's how I want to be remembered by my grandchildren, for the live things that will just keep growing."

We were working on a new field for Remedio, digging a *charco* and ditches to bring water from the wash to the new area he wanted to plant. Remedio, who is now in his sixties, had to give up his old floodwater field two years ago, after a government flood control project cut off his source of stormwaters. He had grown edgy after that, because he felt unable to fulfill his responsibility as a *Tohono O'odham* to tend the earth and help the desert yield its food.

Then a dream came three weeks ago.

"There was my father in a far-off place, offering me some food. When you have a dream like that, and you take the food from someone you knew who is gone, you will be going their way in not too long. That is why I want to fix up this dirt, to make it good for the crops, so that those who live here after me will be able to grow what they need to eat *here* in this place."

That day, Remedio neither planted seeds nor gathered rocks. He simply worked the soil, preparing it for what would come later. His goal was to make *s-kegac jewed*—good earth.

Gary Nabhan

The Gardener

I have loved your hands
small and delicate
have imagined them
braiding my hair
Fingerbones weaving
flowers   Pale skin

brown now   egg speckled
Liver spots you call them
and hide your hands in your lap
Age spots you say
turning them
You would think me foolish
if I told you how often
I want to kiss them
place the back of your hand

against my cheek
feel the warmth
of field's newly turned earth
baby's breath
daisies ready to open
Your hands
stained with sun

Ellen Kort

The Man Born to Farming

The grower of trees, the gardener, the man born to farming,
whose hands reach into the ground and sprout,
to him the soil is a divine drug. He enters into death
yearly, and comes back rejoicing. He has seen the light lie down
in the dung heap, and rise again in the corn.
His thought passes along the row ends like a mole.
What miraculous seed has he swallowed
that the unending sentence of his love flows out of his mouth
like a vine clinging in the sunlight, and like water
descending in the dark?

Wendell Berry

One Man on a Tractor Far Away (excerpt)

Martin ate the meal mostly in silence. But so did he eat all his meals, and so did he live most of his life: in silence.

When he was done, he slipped a toothpick into the corner of his mouth, read aloud a brief devotion for our general benefit, pushed back his chair, stood up, and walked outside.

I followed him. I think I thought I'd talk with him, persuade him of the honor of my intentions. But Martin moved in the sort of solitude that, it seemed to my young self, admitted no foolish intrusions. And once outside, he kept on walking. So I lingered in the yard and watched, following no farther than that.

In twilight the farmer, clad in clean coveralls, strolled westward into the field immediately beyond the yard. He paused. He stood in silhouette, the deep green sky framing his body with such precision that I could see the toothpick twiddling between his lips. His hair was as stiff and wild as a thicket, the great blade of his nose majestic.

Soon Martin knelt on one knee. He reached down and gathered a handful of dirt. He lifted it, then sifted the lumpish dust through his finger onto the palm of his other hand. Suddenly he brought both hands to his face and inhaled. The toothpick got switched to the side; Martin touched the tip of his tongue to the earth. The he rose again. He softly clapped his two hands clean, then slipped them behind the bib of his coveralls, and there he stood, straight up, gazing across the field, his form as black as iron in the gloaming, his elbows forming the joints of folded wings—and I thought: How peaceful! How completely peaceful is this man.

It caused in me a sort of sadness, a nameless elemental yearning.

Walter Wangerin, Jr.

Matmiya

for my Grandmother

I see you sitting
Implanted by roots
Coiled deep from your thighs.
Roots, flesh red, centuries pale.
Hairsprings wound tight
Through fertile earthscapes
Where each layer feeds the next
Into depths immutable.
Though you must rise, must
Move large and slow
When it is time,
O my
Gnarled mother-vine, ancient
As vanished ages,
Your spirit remains
Nourished,
Nourishing me.

I see your figure wrapped in skins
Curved into a mound of earth
Holding your rich dark roots.
Maymiya,
I see you sitting.

Mary TallMountain

Swansonville

for Marcelle

I veer from Beaver Valley onto Swansonville Road
in search of your new home. Our friendship spans ten years
and there's no way I'll let us fade away
quickly as your last address.

I roll down my window
to let the scent of valley in, the green
I swear, greener than in town
where the business of nature's splendor
is business.

A right turn by a one room church . . .
I follow your crinkly map
drawn on the back of a grocery receipt,
savor the sunstruck blackberry vines veiling the curb,
summer apples squashed or standing whole.

I pass easily into the places you live: homey apartment
across from the courthouse, house on Morgan Hill, its view
of our small city, comforting and refined
and this farm, an elixir for my spirit
tired of traffic, tourists, the smell of the paper mill,
the artists keeping score. It's as if, here, there is no muss
that needs editing, no fear
of time lost.

When I walk your garden with its roots
hay-covered, a patch of fenced earth
swelling with lettuce, beans, and radishes
(I didn't *know* grew underground)
I see the bond between you and this land
you mow and weed by hand, this orchard
with fruit hanging just out of reach.

I believe here you will stay
adding years to the heap of compost
holding heat like a furnace, the depths
of all the humid decay, the harvest
and woman
it helps set free.

Mary Lou Sanelli

No Tool or Rope or Pail

It hardly mattered what time of year
We passed by their farmhouse
They never waved,
This old farm couple
Usually bent over in the vegetable garden
Or walking the muddy dooryard
Between house and red weathered barn.
They would look up, see who was passing,
Then look back down ignorant to the event.
We would always wave nonetheless,
Before you dropped me off at work
Further up on the hill,
Toolbox rattling in the backseat,
And then again on the way home
Later in the day, the pale sunlight
High up in their pasture,
Our arms out the window
Cooling ourselves.
And it was that one summer evening
We drove past and caught them sitting
Together on the front porch
At ease, chores done,

The tangle of cats and kittens
Cleaning themselves of fresh spilled milk
On the barn door ramp;
We drove by and they looked up—
The first time I'd ever seen their
Hands free of any work,
No tool or rope or pail—
And they waved.

Bob Arnold

Issa

The man pulling radishes
        pointed the way
with a radish.

Issa
1763-1827

Soaking Up Sun

Today there is the kind of sunshine old men love,
the kind of day when my grandfather would sit
on the south side of the wooden corncrib where
the sunlight warmed slowly all through the day
like a wood stove. One after another dry leaves
fell. No painful memories came. Everything was
lit by a halo of light. The cornstalks glinted bright
as pieces of glass. From the fields and cottonwood
grove came the damp smell of mushrooms, of
things going back to earth. I sat with my grandfather then. Sheep came up to us as we sat there,
their oily wool so warm to my fingers, like a strange
and magic snow. My grandfather whittled sweet
smelling apple sticks just to get at the scent. His
thumb had a permanent groove in it where the
back of the knife blade rested. He let me listen to
the wind, the wild geese, the soft dialect of sheep,
while his own silence taught me every secret thing
he knew.

Tom Hennen

My Father and the Figtree

For other fruits my father was indifferent.
He'd point at the cherry trees and say,
"See those? I wish they were figs."
In the evenings he sat by our beds
weaving folktales like vivid little scarves.
They always involved a figtree.
Even when it didn't fit, he'd stick it in.
Once Joha was walking down the road
and he saw a figtree.
Or, he tied his donkey to a figtree and went to sleep.
Or, later when they caught and arrested him,
his pockets were full of figs.

At age six I ate a dried fig and shrugged.
"That's not what I'm talking about!" he said,
"I'm talking about a fig straight from the earth—
gift of Allah!—on a branch so heavy
it touches the ground.
I'm talking about picking the largest, fattest,
    sweetest fig
in the world and putting it in my mouth."
(Here he'd stop and close his eyes.)

Years passed, we lived in many houses,
none had figtrees.
We had lima beans, zucchini, parsley, beets.
"Plant one!" my mother said,
but my father never did.
He tended garden half-heartedly, forgot to water,
let the okra get too big.
"What a dreamer he is. Look how many
things he starts and doesn't finish."

The last time he moved, I had a phone call,
my father, in Arabic, chanting a song
I'd never heard. "What's that?"
He took me out to the new yard.
There, in the middle of Dallas, Texas,
a tree with the largest, fattest,
sweetest figs in the world.
"It's a figtree song!" he said,
plucking his fruits like ripe tokens,
emblems, assurance
of a world that was always his own.

Naomi Shihab Nye

Earth Dweller

It was all the clods at once become
precious; it was the barn, and the shed,
and the windmill, my hands, the crack
Arlie made in the ax handle: oh, let me stay
here humbly, forgotten, to rejoice in it all;
let the sun casually rise and set.
If I have not found the right place,
teach me; for somewhere inside, the clods are
vaulted mansions, lines through the barn sing
for the saints forever, the shed and windmill
rear so glorious the sun shudders like a gong.

Now I know why people worship, carry around
magic emblems, wake up talking dreams
they teach to their children: the world speaks.
The world speaks everything to us.
It is our only friend.

William Stafford

Rice Lesson

One day I was playing in the mud of a rice field with a half-dozen other little boys. We were catching frogs, racing to see who would be the first to get there. It was a wonderful way to get dirty from head to foot in the shortest possible time. But suddenly we were all scrambling to get out of the paddy. One of the boys had spotted an old man walking across the path toward us. We all knew him and called him "Tata," meaning "grandpa." He was the keeper of the dams. He walked slowly, stooped over a bit as though he were always looking at the ground. Old age is very much respected in India, and we boys shuffled our feet and waited in silence for what we knew was going to be a rebuke.

He came over to us and asked us what we were doing. "Catching frogs," we answered.

He stared down at the churned-up mud and flattened young rice plants in the corner where we had been playing, and I was expecting him to talk about the rice seedlings that we had spoiled. Instead he stooped and scooped up a handful of mud. "What is this?" he asked.

The biggest boy among us took the responsibility of answering for us all. "It's mud, Tata."

"Whose mud is it?" the old man asked.

"It's your mud, Tata. This is your field."

The old man turned and looked at the nearest of the little channels across the dam. "What do you see there, in that channel?" he asked.

"That is water, running over into the lower field," the biggest boy answered.

For the first time Tata looked angry. "Come with me and I will show you water."

We followed him a few steps along the dam, and he pointed to the next channel, where clear water was running. "That is what water looks like," he said. Then he led us back to our nearest channel, and said, "Is that water?"

We hung our heads. "No Tata, that is mud, muddy water," the oldest boy answered. He had heard all this before and did not want to prolong the question-and-answer session, so he hurried on. "And the mud from your field is being carried away to the field below, and it will never come back, because mud always runs downhill, never up again. We are sorry, Tata, and we will never do this again."

But Tata was not ready to stop his lesson as quickly as that, so he went on to tell us that just one handful of mud would grow enough rice for one meal for one person, and it would do it twice a year for years into the future. "That mud flowing over the dam has given my family food every year from long before I was born, and before my grandfather was born. It would have given my grandchildren food, and then given their grandchildren food forever. Now it will never feed us again. When you see mud in the channels of water, you know that life is flowing away from the mountains."

The old man walked slowly back across the path, pausing a moment to adjust with his foot the grass clod in our muddy channel so that no more water flowed through it. We were silent and uncomfortable as we went off to find some other place to play. I had gotten a dose of traditional Indian folk education that would remain with me as long as I lived. Soil was life, and every generation was responsible for preserving it for future generations.

Fred Kirschenmann

Returning from Italy

Clearing customs—
first English spoken in a month
    —do you have anything to declare?

red earth
piece of red rock earth
garlic clove
chestnut from ancestor village

Denise Calvetti Michaels

Ancestral Messengers / Composition 13

no, señora rodriguez
you cannot bring the goat to the 13th floor
you must get rid of the chickens, too
yes, señora, i understand the
goat's fresh milk is best for the baby
but the goat cannot go on the elevator to the 13th floor

of course i'll catch señorita diaz
& her roosters / i know what's going on in 9c

no señora rodriguez, i don't know where
your goat can rest / just not in this building
no, it is not all right to go up the stairs
out of the way of the tenants / oh, please señora
don't try to take the goat to your sister's
house in queens on the e or the f train

it's against the law, señora
how can i tell you the goat is not
against the law / animals are not
against the law / it's just that
living creatures are not welcome here.

Ntozake Shange

Soybeans

The October air was warm and musky, blowing
Over brown fields, heavy with the fragrance
Of freshly combined beans, the breath of harvest.

He was pulling a truckload onto the scales
At the elevator near the rail siding north of town
When a big Cadillac drove up. A man stepped out,
Wearing a three-piece suit and a gold pinky ring.
The man said he had just invested a hundred grand
In soybeans and wanted to see what they looked like.

The farmer stared at the man and was quiet, reaching
For the tobacco in the rear pocket of his jeans,
Where he wore *his* only ring, a threadbare circle rubbed
By working cans of dip and long hours on the backside
Of a hundred acre run. He scooped up a handful
Of small white beans, the pearls of the prairie saying:

Soybeans look like a foot of water on the field in April
When you're ready to plant and can't get in;
Like three kids at the kitchen table
Eating macaroni and cheese five nights in a row;
Or like a broken part on the combine when
Your credit with the implement dealer is nearly tapped.

Soybeans look like prayers bouncing off the ceiling
When prices on the Chicago grain market start to drop;
Or like your old man's tears when you tell him
How much the land might bring for subdivisions.
Soybeans look like the first good night of sleep in weeks
When you unload at the elevator and the kids get Christmas.

He spat a little juice on the tire of the Cadillac,
Laughing despite himself and saying to the man:
Now maybe you can tell me what a hundred grand looks like.

Thomas Alan Orr

Dream Dust

Gather out of Star-dust
Earth-dust
Cloud-dust,
Storm-dust
And splinters of hail,
One handful of Dream-dust
Not for sale.

Langston Hughes

The Transfiguration of Bread

One evening when one thing after another had gone wrong, Mother opened the cupboard door and a dinner plate crashed to the floor and shattered. Enraged by the perfidy of the plate, she pulled the others out of the cupboard one at a time and smashed them to the floor, too. She began demolishing the cups and saucers before she spent her anger. We children, already seated at the table for supper, watched in terror; sometimes Mother took her anger out on us.

She wept, dried her tears, swept up the shards, and served supper in soup bowls. My sisters and I ate in silence, excused ourselves, and went to bed early. For months after that, the family ate everything out of those soup bowls, each meal a reminder, like a festering wound, of that night. There was no money to buy replacement plates. After the harvest, when the money was finally found, we were all able to laugh about such a luxury as new plates, but I never forgot that night, nor, I think, did my mother.

This is one memory I carry of what it means to be poor, but it is not the only one, nor the dominant one. We were, by monetary standards, poor, but we were not, by any reasonable standard of physical need, impoverished.

We worked hard, although not so hard, in fact, as our more modern neighbors. We toiled when the sun was up, rested when it was not, and took Sundays off, while all around us at planting and harvest times the machines rumbled late into the night and Sundays were on their way to becoming ordinary days in the relentless turning of the weeks. As elsewhere in society, our labor-saving machines delivered not so much freedom from drudgery as enslavement to creditors.

Because we raised our own food, we always had an adequate supply; because our fuel was harvested from our own land, we were always warm and dry; because we acquired little, we had little to lose. We experienced such joys and such sorrows as are the lot of all humanity. Our lives were not idyllic—far from it—but neither were they mean or oppressive. Still, it is possible to believe, despite countervailing evidence, that money alone, and only money, can supply life's sufficiencies, or, in the reverse, that to be in want of money is in itself degrading.

One earlier reader of this [story], recalling the dreary novels of Hamlin Garland, reminded me of the "drudgery, tedium, and soul-destroying poverty" of preindustrial rural life and suggested that I was perpetuating "the myth of a golden age in agriculture," "the myth of the cheerful yeomanry," "a pastoral paradise." I don't, in fact, believe in such myths, nor, for that matter, do I know of anybody else who does. These are not myths in any functional sense, but shibboleths. I keenly recall the tedium and drudgery of the life I knew as a child. But my own children, who have grown up in affluence, are also loudly cognizant of the tedium and drudgery of *their* lives. And I remember as do they, many joys and satisfactions. I do not believe that the state of one's soul is in direct relation to the condition of one's bank balance. Wealth is as fully capable of corrupting the soul as poverty.

The primary human-development issues, one would think, have to do with physical and emotional security: do people have shelter from the weather, enough food, clothing adequate to the climate, a reasonable prospect of living to maturity, freedom from random violence? At the next level of development the questions ought to be about achieving one's creative potential: do the physical and emotional circumstances of one's life allow leisure from one's labors—time to love, to dance, to sing, to make poems, to meditate, to play with one's children, to converse with one's friends and neighbors? Only to the extent that money enhances these possibilities, and to the extent that it is equitably distributed in a society, so that the advantages of a few do not oppress the potential of the many, is the accumulation of wealth an appropriate or useful ambition.

The per capita gross product of a nation, often interpreted as a reliable indicator of human health and happiness, is, by such standards, an extremely crude tool. As a measure of comfort of individual lives, it is about as apt, say, as deciding how to dress in the morning according to the mean annual temperature of the region in which one lives. If one lives in the tropics this would work well. But if one lives in Minnesota, where the temperature might be thirty degrees below zero one morning and one hundred degrees above zero another morning, one would be in danger of dying of exposure or of prostration most of the time. The problem with aggregate statistics is that they obscure both extremes and patterns of distribution.

The only acute pain that I can recall suffering because of my family's poverty was the intense humiliation I felt when I discovered, as an adolescent, that most people lived another way and that there was something shameful, so far as others were concerned, about the way we lived. I was embarrassed to invite my friends to our house, which I had thought cozy and warm until I was made to see it as dirty and bare.

Bread was the issue over which we children voiced our new-found shame. Ours was home baked, using wheat raised and ground on the farm, leavened with home-cultured yeast, and sweetened with honey made by the bees we kept at the bottom of our garden. It was fabulous

bread; almost every year it won my mother a purple ribbon at the
Chippewa County fair. The slicing of the first loaf in a new batch, still
steaming, its sweet, nutty aroma filling the kitchen, was one of the
sacred rituals of our household.

But my sisters and I, driven by the collapse of rural society out of
our local school and into the consolidated town school, had tasted the
allure of a new world. We had acquired the preference of the age for
anything manufactured over anything homemade. We suddenly
coveted boughten bread, contrived from flour so denuded of its
essence that its only nutrients came from artificial additives. We were
no longer content to eat hick bread. "Wonder Bread builds strong
bodies seven ways," we said, proud of our familiarity with modern
advertising slogans. We yammered and complained, I am ashamed to
confess, until Mother finally gave up baking bread, and we began to
eat, like modern folk, a factory substitute.

The real poverty that we then experienced, but did not recognize,
characterizes the impoverishment that befell every aspect of rural
culture with the industrialization of farming. Not only our palates
suffered, not only our bodies, deprived of wholesome bread, but our
very souls. Our souls depended in ways we had not anticipated upon
the sanctity of the labors that brought bread to our table. We lost the

ceremony and artfulness, in which every member of the family had some vital role, that once attended the eating of the grain: the planting and tilling, the harvesting and winnowing, the grinding and mixing, the miracle of its rising, the mystery of the transforming fire, the sacrament of the first loaf. Making bread was a critical element in the purpose of our lives, and one of the ways by which we were literally joined to the land. It was at the center of our culture, a civilizing force.

The Latin word from which our *culture* derives has several meanings: to inhabit, to till, to worship; these are, in fact, although we have forgotten it, intimately related actions. To inhabit a place means, if one is attentive to the idea from which the word comes, not simply to occupy it, or merely to own it, but to dwell within it, to have joined oneself in some organic way to it; it is the place where one's heart lives. The word *till* comes from an Old English word meaning to strive after, to get. The word worship is a contraction: it was originally *worth*ship, the homage once paid to whatever one valued. So the idea of culture encompasses not only the arts and inventions of a people, but also the place within which they dwell, all that they strive after, and everything that they find worthy.

When we gave up the baking of bread in our household, we abandoned more than a habit of living; in a subtle but real way, we turned our backs upon our culture; and to that extent our lives became less worshipful. The wholesome mystery of bread, the sacrament of it, I know now, was never in the ingredients but in the labor, and in the laborers who transfigured them into bread.

Paul Gruchow

Follower

My father worked with a horse plough,
His shoulders globed like a full sail strung
Between the shafts and the furrow.
The horses strained at his clicking tongue.

An expert. He would set the wing
And fit the bright-pointed sock.
The sod rolled over without breaking.
At the headrig, with a single pluck

Of reins, the sweating team turned round
And back into the land. His eye
Narrowed and angled at the ground,
Mapping the furrow exactly.

I stumbled in his hobnailed wake,
Fell sometimes on the polished sod;
Sometimes he rode me on his back
Dipping and rising to his plod.

I wanted to grow up and plough,
To close one eye, stiffen my arm.
All I ever did was follow
In his broad shadow around the farm.

I was a nuisance, tripping, falling,
Yapping always. But today
It is my father who keeps stumbling
Behind me, and will not go away.

Seamus Heaney

Fern Hill

Now as I was young and easy under the apple boughs
About the lilting house and happy as the grass was green,
   The night above the dingle starry,
     Time let me hail and climb
    Golden in the heydeys of his eyes,
And honoured among wagons I was prince of the apple towns
And once below a time I lordly had the trees and leaves
     Trail with daisies and barley
   Down the rivers of the windfall light.

  And as I was green and carefree, famous among the barns
About the happy yard and singing as the farm was home,
    In the sun that is young once only,
      Time let me play and be
    Golden in the mercy of his means,
And green and golden I was huntsman and herdsman, the calves
Sang to my horn, the foxes on the hills barked clear and cold,
     And the sabbath rang slowly
   In the pebbles of the holy streams.

All the sun long it was running, it was lovely, the hay
Fields high as the house, the tunes from the chimneys, it was air
    And playing, lovely and watery
     And fire green as grass.

And nightly under the simple stars
As I rode to sleep the owls were bearing the farm away,
All the moon long I heard, blessed among the stables, the night-jars
Flying with the ricks, and the horses
Flashing into the dark.

And then to awake, and the farm, like a wanderer white
With the dew, come back, the cock on his shoulder: it was all
Shining, it was Adam and maiden,
The sky gathered again
And the sun grew round that very day.
So it must have been after the birth of the simple light
In the first, spinning place, the spellbound horses walking warm
Out of the whinnying green stable
On to the fields of praise.

And honoured among foxes and pheasants by the gay house
Under the new made clouds and happy as the heart was long,
In the sun born over and over,
I ran my heedless ways,
My wishes raced through the house high hay
And nothing I cared, at my sky blue trades, that time allows
In all his tuneful turnings so few and such morning songs
Before the children green and golden
Follow him out of grace,

Nothing I cared, in the lamb white days, that time would take me
Up to the swallow thronged loft by the shadow of my hand,
    In the moon that is always rising,
        Nor that riding to sleep
    I should hear him fly with the high fields
And wake to the farm forever fled from the childless land.
Oh as I was young and easy in the mercy of his means,
        Time held me green and dying
    Though I sang in my chains like the sea.

Dylan Thomas

Letter from McCarty's Farm

At first purling of light
I come awake from a
brown velvet dream
horses nosing my arm in the dark
A bird calls outside my window
as I watch the barn
lift the sun up over its head
All week the wind
has been a meticulous gardener here

ruffling green bonnets
of cabbages
pruning edges
lining up rows
of cornstalks
bleached blond
by an early freeze
The pond thirsty now
from years of drought
still dances with herons
one last reminder
of the lake it used to be

Wave after wave of geese
fill the sky
in great V's
as if this letter
we've learned to love
is flying out
from the alphabet
I stroke the bones
of a dead maple
see where the woodpile
is stitched together by spiders

Today I saw
early morning frosty on the backs
of brown and white horses
watched a cat
circle the field
walking the middle rail
of wooden fence
and last night the moon
whittled everything to slivers
the ridge the strip of grassland

If it's true
that landscape
is to be read as text
I will take it as wafer
The whole complete
roundness of it
place it on my tongue

Ellen Kort

Work That Is Real

The beginning of art—
a rice-planting song
in the backcountry.

—*Bashō*
1644-1694

To be of use

The people I love the best
jump into work head first
without dallying in the shallows
and swim off with sure strokes almost out of sight.
They seem to become natives of that element,
the black sleek heads of seals
bouncing like half-submerged balls.

I love people who harness themselves, an ox to a heavy cart,
who pull like water buffalo, with massive patience,
who strain in the mud and the muck to move things forward,
who do what has to be done, again and again.

I want to be with people who submerge
in the task, who go into the fields to harvest
and work in a row and pass the bags along,
who stand in the line and haul in their places,
who are not parlor generals and field deserters
but move in a common rhythm
when the food must come in or the fire be put out.

The work of the world is common as mud.
Botched, it smears the hands, crumbles to dust.
But the thing worth doing well done
has a shape that satisfies, clean and evident.

Greek amphoras for wine or oil,
Hopi vases that held corn, are put in museums
but you know they were made to be used.
The pitcher cries for water to carry
and a person for work that is real.

Marge Piercy

Planting Onions

It is right
that I fall to my knees
on this damp, stony cake,
that I bend my back
and bow my head.

Sun warms my shoulders,
the nape of my neck,
and the air is tangy with rot.
Bulbs rustle like spirits
in their sack.

I bury each one
a trowel's width under.
May they take hold,
rising green in time
to help us weep and live.

Jane Flanders

Manifesto: The Mad Farmer Liberation Front

Love the quick profit, the annual raise,
vacation with pay. Want more
of everything ready-made. Be afraid
to know your neighbors and to die.
And you will have a window in your head
Not even your future will be a mystery
any more. Your mind will be punched in a card
and shut away in a little drawer.
When they want you to buy something
they will call you. When they want you
to die for profit they will let you know.
So, friends, every day do something
that won't compute. Love the Lord.
Love the world. Work for nothing.
Take all that you have and be poor.
Love someone who does not deserve it.
Denounce the government and embrace
the flag. Hope to live in that free
republic for which it stands.
Give your approval to all you cannot
understand. Praise ignorance, for what man
has not encountered he has not destroyed.

Ask the questions that have no answers.
Invest in the millennium. Plant sequoias.
Say that your main crop is the forest
that you did not plant,
that you will not live to harvest.
Say that the leaves are harvested
when they have rotted into the mold.
Call that profit. Prophesy such returns.
Put your faith in the two inches of humus
that will build under the trees
every thousand years.
Listen to carrion—put your ear
close, and hear the faint chattering
of the songs that are to come.
Expect the end of the world. Laugh.
Laughter is immeasurable. Be joyful
though you have considered all the facts.
So long as women do not go cheap
for power, please women more than men.
Ask yourself: Will this satisfy
a woman satisfied to bear a child?
Will this disturb the sleep

of a woman near to giving birth?
Go with your love to the fields.
Lie easy in the shade. Rest your head
in her lap. Swear allegiance
to what is nighest your thoughts.
As soon as the generals and the politicos
can predict the motions of your mind,
lose it. Leave it as a sign
to mark the false trail, the way
you didn't go. Be like the fox
who makes more tracks than necessary,
some in the wrong direction.
Practice resurrection.

Wendell Berry

Putting in the Seed

You come to fetch me from my work tonight
When supper's on the table, and we'll see
If I can leave off burying the white
Soft petals fallen from the apple tree
(Soft petals, yes, but not so barren quite,
Mingled with these, smooth bean and wrinkled pea),
And go along with you ere you lose sight
Of what you came for and become like me,
Slave to a springtime passion for the earth.
How Love burns through the Putting in the Seed
On through the watching for that early birth
When, just as the soil tarnishes with weed,
The sturdy seedling with arched body comes
Shouldering its way and shedding the earth crumbs.

Robert Frost

The Seed Cutters

They seem hundreds of years away. Brueghel,
You'll know them if I can get them true.
They kneel under the hedge in a half-circle
Behind a windbreak wind is breaking through.
They are the seed cutters. The tuck and frill
Of leaf-sprout is on the seed potatoes
Buried under that straw. With time to kill,
They are taking their time. Each sharp knife goes
Lazily halving each root that falls apart
In the palm of the hand: a milky gleam,
And, at the centre, a dark watermark.
Oh, calendar customs! Under the broom
Yellowing over them, compose the frieze
With all of us there, our anonymities.

Seamus Heaney

"What crops the region will bear . . ."

In early spring, when the ice on the snowy mountains
Melts and the west wind loosens and crumbles the clods,
Then it's high time for my bull at the deep-driven plough
To groan, and the share to gleam with the furrow's polishing.
That field and that alone
Answers the prayer of the demanding farmer
Which twice has felt the sun and twice the cold;
Its superabundant harvest burst his barns.
But with untried land, before we cleave it with iron,
We must con its varying moods of wind and sky
With care—the place's native style and habit,
What crops the region will bear and what refuse.
Here corn will prosper better, there the grape,
Elsewhere young trees or greenery unbidden . . .

Excerpts from The Georgics of Virgil *(26 B.C.)*
translated by L. P. Wilkinson

The Meadow

We have welded the towbar
and turned the mower's eighteen blades –
the mower, the meadow reiver.
We'll work all night, by the last
and first light and, in between, by the minutes
of moonlight. This is hay fever.

For weeks we've watched smudged fields
weighted down by mean July.
We've heard them broadcast
brightness and woken to wet weather.
We'd be better off watching Billy McNamee
than paying heed to the radio forecast.

When meadows grow he finds a way.
We say we'll trust our own translation
of the sky and start to mow
this evening. We'll be racing the rain.
Tomorrow we'll turn and turn again.
Midweek we'll set the bob to row.

Then we'll bale. We did that then,
headed the stacks with loose hay
from the headlands. We thought we'd won

until we heard of loss that rotted in rows
and stopped aftergrass. Insult to injury.
Talk everywhere of fusty fodder, self-combustion.

Ten years ago we built ten thousand bales,
two of us, and climbed the mountain
afterwards to rest in forestry that mearns
sheep pasture, a famine field
of lazy beds. We gazed down from
a cemetery of thirty cairns
across a stonewalled country.
Stack of bales in circles – our work
stood out like harvest monoliths.
A thousand stones, standing,
speaking, leaning, lying stones,
the key – and cornerstones of myths . . .

Our farms began in those.
It was as if we tried to read the signs
of Newgrange from the moon. A thistle splinter
brought us back to earth
knowing that we'd gathered of its plenty
enough to fortify our care against the winter.

Peter Fallon

Tarry Flynn

On an apple-ripe September morning
Through the mist-chill fields I went
With a pitch-fork on my shoulder
Less for use than devilment.

The threshing mill was set-up, I knew,
In Cassidys' haggard last night,
And we owed them a day at the threshing
Since last year. O it was delight

To be paying bills of laughter
And chaffy gossip in kind
With work thrown in to ballast
The fantasy-soaring mind.

As I crossed the wooden bridge I wondered
As I looked into the drain
If ever a summer morning should find me
Shoveling up eels again.

And I thought of the wasps' nest in the bank
And how I got chased one day
Leaving the drag and the scraw-knife behind,
How I covered my face with hay

The wet leaves of the cocksfoot
Polished my boots as I
Went round by the glistening bog-holes
Lost in unthinking joy.

I'll be carrying bags today, I mused,
The best job at the mill
With plenty of time to talk of our loves
As we wait for the bags to fill.

Maybe Mary might call round . . .
And then I came to the haggard gate,
And I knew as I entered that I had come
Through fields that were part of no earthly estate.

Patrick Kavanaugh

After Apple Picking

My long two-pointed ladder's sticking through a tree
Toward heaven still,
And there's a barrel that I didn't fill
Beside it, and there may be two or three
Apples I didn't pick upon some bough.
But I am done with apple-picking now.
Essence of winter sleep is on the night,
The scent of apples: I am drowsing off.
I cannot rub the strangeness from my sight
I got from looking through a pane of glass
I skimmed this morning from the drinking trough
And held against the world of hoary grass.
It melted, and I let it fall and break.
But I was well
Upon my way to sleep before it fell,
And I could tell
What form my dreaming was about to take.
Magnified apples appear and disappear,
Stem end and blossom end,
And every fleck of russet showing clear.
My instep arch not only keeps the ache,
It keeps the pressure of a ladder-round.
I feel the ladder sway as the boughs bend.

And I keep hearing from the cellar bin
The rumbling sound
Of load on load of apples coming in.
For I have had too much
Of apple-picking: I am overtired
Of the great harvest I myself desired.
There were ten thousand thousand fruit to touch,
Cherish in hand, lift down, and not let fall.
For all
That struck the earth,
No matter if not bruised or spiked with stubble,
Went surely to the cider-apple heap
As of no worth.
One can see what will trouble
This sleep of mine, whatever sleep it is.
Were he not gone,
The woodchuck could say whether it's like his
Long sleep, as I describe its coming on,
Or just some human sleep.

Robert Frost

Chores

All day he's shoveled green pine sawdust
out of the trailer truck into the chute.
From time to time he's clambered down to even
the pile. Now his hair is frosted with sawdust.
Little rivers of sawdust pour out of his boots.

I hope in the afterlife there's none of this stuff
he says, stripping nude in the late September sun
while I broom off his jeans, his sweater flocked
with granules, his immersed-in-sawdust socks.
I hope there's no bedding, no stalls, no barn

no more repairs to the paddock gate the horses
burst through when snow avalanches off the roof.
Although the old broodmare, our first foal, is his,
horses, he's fond of saying, make divorces.
fifty years married, he's safely facetious.

No garden pump that's airbound, no window a grouse
flies into and shatters, no ancient tractor's
intractable problem with carburetor
ignition or piston, no mowers and no chain saws
that refuse to start, or start, misfire and quit.

But after a Bloody Mary on the terrace
already frost-heaved despite our heroic efforts
to level the bricks a few years back, he says
let's walk up to the field and catch the sunset
and off we go, a couple of aging fools.

I hope, he says, on the other side there's a lot
less work, but just in case I'm bringing tools.

Maxine Kumin

Ox Cart Man

In October of the year,
he counts potatoes dug from the brown field,
counting the seed, counting
the cellar's portion out,
and bags the rest on the cart's floor.

He packs wool sheared in April, honey
in combs, linen, leather
tanned from deerhide,
and vinegar in a barrel
hooped by hand at the forge's fire.

He walks by ox's head, ten days
to Portsmouth Market, and sells potatoes,
and the bag that carries potatoes,
flaxseed, birch brooms, maple sugar, goose
feathers, yarn.

When the cart is empty he sells the cart.
When the cart is sold he sells the ox,
harness and yoke, and walks
home, his pockets heavy
with the year's coin for salt and taxes,

and at home by fire's light in November cold
stitches new harness
for next year's ox in the barn,
and carves the yoke, and saws planks
building the cart again.

Donald Hall

Those Mornings

My father's Holsteins
stood shoulder to
shoulder in the fenced-in
yard, anomalies
taking shape in
the coming
light. Their slow
and steady breathing, rising
smoke in the air, like factories
along the river, firing-up at the start
of day. Inside we
wander the stanchions, whitewashed
timbers, thick and heavy in our own
desires, milking the future
our lives would surely
resemble, years from now,
not this, not here in this
nothingness of farm. When we
open the doors, the cows,
surge and enter, warm,
ready, alive.

Robert Kinsley

An Ox Looks at Man

They are more delicate even than shrubs and they run
and run from one side to the other, always forgetting
something. Surely they lack I don't know what
basic ingredient, though they present themselves
as noble or serious, at times. Oh, terribly serious,
even tragic. Poor things, one would say that they hear
neither the song of air nor the secrets of hay;
likewise they seem not to see what is visible
and common to each of us, in space. And they are sad,
and in the wake of sadness they come to cruelty.
All their expression lives in their eyes—and loses itself
to a simple lowering of lids, to a shadow.
And since there is little of the mountain about them—
nothing in the hair or in the terribly fragile limbs
but coldness and secrecy—it is impossible for them
to settle themselves into forms that are calm, lasting,
and necessary. They have, perhaps, a kind
of melancholy grace (one minute) and with this they allow
themselves to forget the problems and translucent
inner emptiness that make them so poor and so lacking
when it comes to uttering silly and painful sounds:
    desire, love, jealousy
(what do we know?)—sounds that scatter and fall in the field
like troubled stones and burn the herbs and the water,
and after this it is hard to keep chewing away at our truth.

Carlos Drummond de Andrade
translation by Mark Strand

Um boi vê os homens

Tão delicados (mais que um arbusto) e correm
e correm de um para outro lado, sempre esquecidos
de alguma coisa. Certamente, falha-lhes
não sei que atributo essencial, posto se apresentem nobres
e graves, por vezes. Ah, espantosamente graves,
até sinistro. Coitados, dir-se-ia não escutam
nem o canto do ar nem os segredos de feno,
como também parecem não enxergar o que é visível
e comum a cada um de nós, no espaço. E ficam tristes
e no rasto de tristeza chegam à crueldade.
Toda a expressão deles mora nos olhos—e perde-se
a um simples baixir de cílios, a uma sombra.
Nada nos pêlos, nos extremos de inconcebível fragilidade,
e como neles há ponca montanha,
e que secura e que reentrâncias e que
impossibilidade de se organizarem em formas calmas,
permanentes e necessárias. Têm, talvez,
certa graça melancólica (um minuto) e com isto se fazem
perdoar a agitação incómoda e o translúcido
vazio interior que os torna tão pobres e carecidos
de emitir sons absurdos e agônicos; desejo, amor, ciúme
(que sabemos nós?) sons que se despedaçam e tombam no campo
como pedras aflitas e queimam a erva e a água,
e difícil, depois disto, é ruminarmos nossa verdade.

Carlos Drummond de Andrade

Surrender

Restless, I go down to the barn and attempt to dissect the concept of "peace . . ."

As I help Anna clean out the lambing pens, my skirt pinned up under an apron, mind and body begin to alter their usual relation to each other. I cannot think about "peace"; I cannot think about anything. This is a natural consequence of doing the kind of repetitive work called "mindless" by those who disdain it. Yet my mind is not so much absent as still. It's not at its usual station in my head, but diffused through my body. Or, slide beyond the body, even, to encompass all that's going on in the barn.

My hands are efficiently chucking down clean straw and, as I watch the ewe position herself for the scrambling lamb, my nipples contract in the reflex of a nursing mother. If I were not well past the childbearing years, my blouse might be soaked with milk. This is a passing, negligible sensation, a product of merely being present. I do not stop working to examine it. A casual dissolution of boundaries body-to-body happens when you work in the barn. With animals, it's safe, and pertinent, to have no edges. It helps you to manage sheep and them to manage you. If I bother to retrieve my mind, I find it shared out among the ewes, who have made good time with it.

There is deep rest in this loss of self. Peace, which implies stillness, and ecstasy: every hair in motion. Thus lovers and people who read each other's poems breathe the other, if they love or read well. Thus music. If you play the fiddle, no matter how badly, and you go to hear a great violinist—as last month I went to a concert of Isaac Stern's—you hear the performance in the hollows of your own body (or has it ceased to be your body?) that lilt of Stern's at the tip of the bow is in your fingers. If I am flowing in this moment through one pride of skin and not another, it's accident. And I test the limits of this bubble as once I tested the limits of the womb.

When you go down to the lambing pens you can tell from the doorway if something's gone wrong: a ewe whose lamb is dead will have slipped back in the fold with her sisters. Most animals are pragmatic and have little patience with weakness—perhaps you have seen how a mother cat will favor her strong, aggressive kitten and paw aside the runts. Last night Anna struggled till 3 a.m. to save a lamb too short to reach the teats, tubing colostrum into her stomach, then bottle feeding every two hours. This morning the lamb came to me with her tail shaking, a sign of health, and took two ounces of formula. In the barnyard, I try to volunteer a shift with Anna, sparing her the night work since I'm fresher.

But—"I don't think we will have to stay up tonight," she says. Her tone is the oblique and respectful one used by my dad and his pilot friends when refusing to pronounce the word *crash*. Over her shoulder I see four ewes in the fold where three had been standing.

We put the dead lamb in a plastic bucket, later to bury. "Poor little mauser, "says Anna. "Still, she had some good hours."

Philosophers make distinctions between varieties of dispossession; it cannot be the same, they say, to surrender to love, to music, to animal creation, and to prayer. (But stand with someone you love, palm to palm, eyes closed, and sing a perfect fourth . . .) Since I experience these slips of consciousness as similar, I can only speak from what I know. Intensity of presence is the common element, though in the next moment one could say, intensity of absence.

Without presence, the violence would be unthinkable: of God, of Zen practice, of lovemaking, and certainly of the farm. How disquieting to fight so hard for the life of a lamb and tomorrow meet its cousin tucked up in the crockpot. *Namaste*: I honor the god in you.

Mary Rose O'Reilley

Girl on a Tractor

I knew the names of all the cows before
I knew my alphabet, but no matter the
subject, I had mastery of it, and when
it came time to help in the fields, I
learned to drive a tractor at just the right
speed, so that two men, walking
on either side of the moving wagon
could each lift a bale, walk towards
the steadily arriving platform and
simultaneously hoist the hay onto
the rack, walk to the next bale, lift,
turn, and find me there, exactly where
I should be, my hand on the throttle,
carefully measuring out the pace.

Joyce Sutphen

Names of Horses

All winter your brute shoulders strained against collars, padding
and steerhide over the ash hames, to haul
sledges of cordwood for drying through spring and summer,
for the Glenwood stove next winter, and for the simmering range.

In April you pulled cartloads of manure to spread on the fields,
dark manure of Holsteins, and knobs of your own clustered with
     oats.
All summer you mowed the grass in the meadow and hayfield, the
    mowing machine
clacketing beside you, while the sun walked high in the morning;

and after noon's heat, you pulled a clawed rake through the same
    acres,
gathering stacks, and dragged the wagon from stack to stack,
and the built hayrack back, uphill to the chaffy barn,
three loads of hay a day, hanging wide from the hayrack.

Sundays you trotted the two miles to church with the light load
of a leather quartertop buggy, and grazed in the sound of hymns.
Generation on generation, your neck rubbed the window sill
of the stall, smoothing the wood as the sea smooths glass.

When you were old and lame, when your shoulders hurt bending
    to graze,
one October the man, who fed you and kept you, and harnessed you
    every morning,
led you through corn stubble to sandy ground above Eagle Pond,
and dug a hole beside you where you stood shuddering in your skin,

and lay the shotgun's muzzle in the boneless hollow behind your
    ear,
and fired the slug into your brain, and felled you into your grave,
shoveling sand to cover you, setting goldenrod upright above you,
where by next summer a dent in the ground made your monument.

For a hundred and fifty years, in the pasture of dead horses,
roots of pine trees pushed through the pale curves of your ribs,
yellow blossoms flourished above you in autumn, and in winter
frost heaved your bones in the ground   old toilers, soil makers:

O Roger, Mackerel, Riley, Ned, Nellie, Chester, Lady Ghost.

Donald Hall

Why I Make the Best Barrels

Last week, the old men drove out from the winery
to tell me that I make the best barrels they have ever used.
They seemed surprised, since there were no women coopers
in my father's generation, or the generations before.
I told them that nothing has changed; they watched me
do the work by hand, content to stand as shavings
and sawdust piled up on their polished boots. While I worked,
I tried to explain to them what my father taught me,
about working with wood, about the art, about the years
learning wood, learning where and how to shape the perfect stave.
It is meticulous work, to make twenty-four planks of white oak
slim at the ends and wide in the middle, to fit them together
in a perfect watertight bulge, like a body, the abdomen growing
as I tighten hoops, bind the staves together. I am the best
because I understand how something flat and straight can curve
as it matures. And I can construct the perfect container for aging wine,
red like the blood that nourishes my unborn child.

Eliza Garza

The seven of pentacles

Under a sky the color of pea soup
she is looking at her work growing away there
actively, thickly like grapevines or pole beans
as things grow in the real world, slowly enough.
If you tend them properly, if you mulch, if you water,
if you provide birds that eat insects a home and winter food,
if the sun shines and you pick off caterpillars,
if the praying mantis comes and the ladybugs and the bees,
then the plants flourish, but at their own internal clock.

Connections are made slowly, sometimes they grow underground.
You cannot tell always by looking what is happening.
More than half a tree is spread out in the soil under your feet.
Penetrate quietly as the earthworm that blows no trumpet.
Fight persistently as the creeper that brings down the tree.
Spread like the squash plant that overruns the garden.
Gnaw in the dark and use the sun to make sugar.

Weave real connections, create real nodes, build real houses.
Live a life you can endure: make love that is loving.
Keep tangling and interweaving and taking more in,
a thicket and bramble wilderness to the outside but to us
interconnected with rabbit runs and burrows and lairs.

Live as if you liked yourself, and it may happen:
reach out, keep reaching out, keep bringing in.
This is how we are going to live for a long time: not always,
for every gardener knows that after the digging, after the planting,
after the long season of tending and growth, the harvest comes.

Marge Piercy

Primary Lessons in Political Economy

For every ten bushels of paddy she harvests
    the landless laborer takes home one.

This woman, who name is Hiria, would have to starve
    for three days to buy a liter of milk.

If she were to check her hunger and not eat
    for a month, she could buy a book of poems.

And if Hiria, who works endlessly, could starve
    endlessly, in ten years she could buy that piece

Of land on which during short winter evenings
    the landlord's son plays badminton.

Amitava Kumar

Butterflies

The grandmother plaited her granddaughter's hair and then she said, "Get your lunch. Put it in your bag. Get your apple. You come straight back after school, straight home here. Listen to the teacher," she said. "Do what she say."

Her grandfather was out on the step. He walked down the path with her and out onto the footpath. He said to a neighbor, "Our granddaughter goes to school. She lives with us now."

"She's fine," the neighbor said. "She's terrific with her two plaits in her hair."

"And clever," the grandfather said. "Writes every day in her book."

"She's fine," the neighbor said.

The grandfather waited with his granddaughter by the crossing and then he said, "Go to school. Listen to the teacher. Do what she say."

When the granddaughter came home from school her grandfather was hoeing around the cabbages. Her grandmother was picking beans. They stopped their work.

"You bring your book home?" the grandmother asked.

"Yes."

"You write your story?"

"Yes."

"What's your story?"

"About the butterflies."

"Get your book then. Read your story."

The granddaughter took her book from her schoolbag and opened it.

"I killed all the butterflies," she read. "This is me and this is all the butterflies," she read.

"And your teacher like your story, did she?"

"I don't know."

"What your teacher say?"

"She said butterflies are beautiful creatures. They hatch out and fly in the sun. The butterflies visit all the pretty flowers, she said. They lay their eggs and then they die. You don't kill butterflies, that's what she said."

The grandmother and the grandfather were quiet for a long time, and their granddaughter, holding the book, stood quite still in the warm garden.

"Because you see," the grandfather said, "your teacher, she buy all her cabbages from the supermarket and that's why."

Patricia Grace

Kneeling Here, I Feel Good

Sand: crystalline children
of dead mountains.
Little quartz worlds
rubbed by the wind.

Compost: rich as memory
sediment of our pleasures,
orange rinds and roses and beef bones,
coffee and cork and dead lettuce,
trimmings of hair and lawn.

I marry you, I marry you.
In your mingling under my grubby nails
I touch the seeds of what will be.
Revolution and germination
are mysteries of birth
without which
many
are born to starve.

I am kneeling and planting.
I am making fertile.
I am putting
some of myself
back in the soil.
Soon enough
sweet black mother of our food
you will have the rest.

Marge Piercy

Worms of Mystery

Worms of mystery sneak through the mud
giving magic and courage to the garden.

Corn sprouts up with promise
making the sun explode with light
as the worms inch back
to their homes under the crops
and stand proudly
on the face of the earth.

Elise Greiner, 3rd grade

Worms

Worms—
they jump through fields of wonder
like boats floating through a river.
They doctor the plans of gardens
like fish swimming in a lake.
At night, the worms go to sleep
after a hard day working,
and dream about carrots,
celery, broccoli, and mud.

LaDonna Wilson, 3rd grade

Apotheosis of the Kitchen Goddess II

There is a goddess and I know her. Her hands are not clean,
And she is large and strong and not too young. She wears
A sweatshirt with a hood and jeans, and sells black-purple
Eggplant, spinach, bright broccoli, sixty cents
The pound at the Greenmarket at Union Square. Her slat-side truck
Has Pennsylvania plates, and she says she lives near Lancaster.
But I know the truth, because her calloused hands turn earth
To things good to eat, and green, and lovely.

Teresa Noelle Roberts

Making Tortillas

My body remembers
what it means to love slowly,
what it means to start
from scratch:
to soak the maíz,
scatter bonedust in the limewater,
and let the seeds soften
overnight.

Sunrise is the best time
for grinding masa,
cormeal rolling out
on the metate like a flannel sheet.
Smell of wet corn, lard, fresh
morning love and the light
sound of clapping

       Pressed between the palms,
clap-clap
      thin yellow moons—
clap-clap
      still moist, heavy still
      from last night's soaking

clap-clap
             slowly start finding their shape.
clap-clap.

My body remembers
the feel of the griddle,
beads of grease sizzling
under the skin, a cry gathering
like an air bubble in the belly
of the unleavened cake. Smell
of baked tortillas all over the house,
all over the hands still
hot from clapping, cooking.
Tortilleras, we are called,
grinders of maíz, makers, bakers,
slow lovers of women.
The secret is starting from scratch.

Alicia Gaspar De Alba

Potatoes

This is the month of warm days
and a spirit of ice
that breathes in the dark,
the month we dig potatoes
small as a child's fist.
Under soil, light skins
and lifeline to leaves and sun.

It is the way this daughter stands beside me
in close faith that I am warm
that makes me remember
so many years of the same work
preparing for quiet winter,
old women bent with children
in dusty fields.

All summer the potatoes have grown
in silence,
gentle,
moving stones away.

And my daughter has changed this way.
So many things to say to her
but our worlds are not the same.
I am the leaves, above ground in the sun
and she is small, dark,
clinging to buried roots,
holding tight to leaves.

In one day of digging the earth,
there is communion
of things we remember
and forget.
We taste starch
turn to sugar in our mouths.

Linda Hogan

A Recipe for a Garden

Throw in some soil,
create some labels
and water by the power of the sun.

Sprinkle every dry day,
and dig holes for seeds to come into flowers.
Add roses and a huge stretch for tulips.
Pinch in a bowl of knowledge.
Hope for daisies to grow.

Combine bravery with it
to come up with corn, peas, potatoes,
tomatoes, and strawberries.
Add a net for crows.
Then, continue so it comes to life.

Now make one more garden.

Henry Phillips, 2nd grade

At the Table

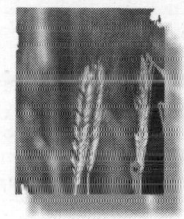

Bread is the warmest,
kindest of words.
Write it always with a capital letter,
like your own name.

Russian café sign

Wheat

Let a stalk of wheat
be your witness
to every difficult day.
Since it was a flame
before it was a plant,
since it was courage
before it was grain,
since it was determination
before it was growth,
and, above all, since it was prayer
before it was fruition,
it has nothing to point to
but the sky.
Remember the incredibly gentle wheat stalk
which holds its countless arrows fixed
to shoot from the bowstring—
you, standing in the same position
where the wind holds it.

Ishihara Yoshiro

A Pot of Red Lentils

simmers on the kitchen stove.
All afternoon dense kernels
surrender to the fertile
juices, their tender bellies
swelling with delight.

In the yard we plant
rhubarb, cauliflower, artichokes,
cupping wet earth over tubers,
our labor the germ
of later sustenance and renewal.

Across the field the sound of a baby crying
as we carry in the last carrots,
whorls of butter lettuce,
a basket of red potatoes.

I want to remember us this way—
late September sun streaming through
the window, bread loaves and golden
bunches of grapes on the table,
spoonfuls of hot soup rising
to our lips, filling us
with what endures.

Peter Pereira

Grace

Thanks & blessing be
to the Sun & the Earth
for this bread & this wine,
        this fruit, this meat, this salt.
            this food;
thanks be & blessing to them
who prepare it, who serve it;
thanks & blessing to them
who share it
        (& also the absent & the dead).
Thanks & blessing to them who bring it
        (may they not want),
to them who plant & tend it,
harvest & gather it
        (may they not want);
thanks & blessing to them who work
        & blessing to them who cannot;
may they not want – for their hunger
        sours the wine & robs
            the taste from the salt.
Thanks be for the sustenance & strength
for our dance & the work of justice, of peace.

Rafael Jesus González

Ode to the Apple

Oda a la manzama

You, apple,
are the object
of my praise.
I want to fill
my mouth
with your name.
I want to eat you whole.

You are always
fresh, like nothing
and nobody,
You have always
just fallen
from Paradise:
dawn's
rosy cheek
full
and perfect!

Compared
to you
the fruits of the earth
are
so awkward:

A ti, manzana,
quiero
celebrarte
llenándome
con tu nombre
la boca,
comiéndote.

Siempre
eres nueva como nada
o nadie,
siempre
recién caida
del Paraíso:
plena
y pura
mejilla arrebolada
de la aurora!

Qué difíciles
son
comparados
contigo
los frutos de la tierra

bunchy grapes,
mangos,
bony
plums, and submerged figs.
You are pure balm,
fragrant bread,
the cheese
of all that flowers.

When we bite into
your round innocence
we too regress
for a moment
to the state
of the newborn:
there's still some apple in us all.

I want
total abundance,
your family
multiplied.
I want
a city,
a republic,

las celulares uvas,
los mangos,
tenebrosos, las huesudas
ciruelas, los higos submarinos:
tú eres pomada pura,
pan fragante,
queso
de la vegetación.

Cuando mordemos
tu redonda inocencia
volvemos
por un instante
a ser
también recién creadas criaturas:
aún tenemos algo de manzana.

Yo quiero
una abundancia
total, la multiplicación
de tu familia
quiero
una ciudad,
una república,

a Mississippi River
of apples,
and I want to see
gathered on its banks
the world's
entire
population
united and reunited
in the simplest act we know;
I want us to bite into an apple.

un rio Mississippi
de manzanas,
y en sus orillas
quiero ver
a toda
la población
del mundo
unida, reunida,
en el acto más simple de la tierra:
mordiendo una manzana.

Pablo Neruda
translation by Ken Krabbenhoft

From Blossoms

From blossoms comes
this brown paper bag of peaches
we bought from the boy
at the bend in the road where we turned toward
signs painted Peaches.

From laden boughs, from hands,
from sweet fellowship in the bins,
comes nectar at the roadside, succulent
peaches we devour, dusty skin and all,
comes the familiar dust of summer, dust we eat.

O, to take what we love inside,
to carry within us an orchard, to eat
not only the skin, but the shade,
not only the sugar, but the days, to hold
the fruit in our hands, adore it, then bite into
the round jubilance of peach.

There are days we live
as if death were nowhere
in the background, from joy
to joy to joy, from wing to wing,
from blossom to blossom to
impossible blossom, to sweet impossible blossom.

Li-Young Lee

916
—

His feet are shod with Gauze –
His Helmet, is of Gold,
His Breast, a Single Onyx
With Chrysophrase, inlaid.

His Labor is a Chant –
His Idleness – a Tune –
Oh, for a Bee's experience
Of Clovers, and of Noon!

Emily Dickinson

Bees
—

The bees joke about the fun
they had making honey.
They give the honey
that provides life to all living things.
Their home is in a tree,
and their honey is as majestic
as gold.

Dean Shumway, 3rd grade

August

The opposing
of peach and sugar,
and the sun inside the afternoon
like the stone in the fruit.

The ear of corn keeps
its laughter intact, yellow and firm.

August.
The little boys eat
brown bread and delicious moon.

Frederico Garcia Lorca

"Vegetables make love above the tenors—"

from Under Milk Wood

Vegetables make love
above the tenors
where only dogs can hear,
those carnivorous curs
who occasionally take
a jolt of grain or carrot.

Vegetables,
with their lascivious root
plunged into wormed dirt,
loving   soundlessly,
tendrils reaching to moist,
good earth,   singing
in dark stunned caves
above the whine of bats.

Oh, round, red, ruddy beet,
stain my hungry chin
with remembered passion.

Nancy Talley

cutting greens

curling them around
i hold their bodies in obscene embrace
thinking of everything but kinship.
collards and kale
strain against each strange other
away from my kissmaking hand and
the iron bedpot.
the pot is black,
the cutting board is black,
my hand,
and just for a minute
the greens roll black under the knife,
and the kitchen twists dark on its spine
and i taste in my natural appetite
the bond of live things everywhere.

Lucille Clifton

Dandelion Greens

You must come back, as your grandmother did,
with her basket and sharp knife, in daffodil light,
to the pasture, where the best greens spring
from heaps of dung, dark in the still brown
meadow grass. Cut them close to the root,
before they flower, rinse them in rain water
and bring them to the table, tossed
with oil, vinegar and salt, or homemade dressing.

They will be bitter but rich in iron—
your spring tonic, your antidote to sleep.
Eat them because they are good for you.
Eat them in joy, for the earth revives.
Eat them in remembrance of your grandmother,
who raised ten children on them. Think
of all the dandelions they picked for her,
the countless downy seeds their laughter spread.

This is the life we believe in—
the saw-toothed blades, the lavish, common flowers.

Jane Flanders

The First Green of Spring

Out walking in the swamp picking cowslip, marsh marigold,
this sweet first green of spring. Now sautéed in a pan melting
to a deeper green than ever they were alive, this green, this life,

harbinger of things to come. Now we sit at the table munching
on this message from the dawn which says we and the world
are alive again today, and this is the world's birthday. And

even though we know we are growing old, we are dying, we
will never be young again, we also know we're still right here
now, today, and, my oh my! don't these greens taste good.

David Budbill

From the Market

Come, radishes, rosy against your greens,
crisp when I am soft with weakness.

Oh what voluptuaries you are! yet
with the definitive sharpness of the scissors.

Ambition dances about you,
yet you are totally unmoved, like true

emissaries of red.

I, what there is of me, may be argued:
but you may not. Your whole self struts;
your leafiness flutters above your head
like a crown of doves.

No radish was ever terrified.

How you cheer me, strong souls for a dime.

Sandra McPherson
Excerpt from Three from the Market

Ode to the Onion

Onion,
shining flask,
your beauty assembled
petal by petal,
they affixed crystal scales to you
and your belly of dew grew round
in the secret depth of the dark earth.
The miracle took place
underground,
and when your lazy green stalk
appeared
and your leaves were born
like swords in the garden,
the earth gathered its strength
exhibiting your naked transparency,
and just as the distant sea
copied the magnolia in Aphrodite
raising up her breasts,
so the earth
made you,
onion,
as bright as a planet

Oda a la cebolla

Cebolla,
luminosa redoma,
pétalo a pétalo
se formó tu hermosura,
escamas de cristal te acrecentaron
y en el secreto de la tierra oscura
se redondeó tu vientre de rocío.
Bajo la tierra
fue el milagro
y cuando apareció
tu torpe tallo verde,
y nacieron
tus hojas como espadas en el huerto,
la tierra acumuló su poderío
mostrando tu desnuda transparencia,
y como en Afrodita el mar remoto
duplicó la magnolia
levantando sus senos,
la tierra
así te hizo,
cebolla,
clara como un planeta,

and fated
to shine,
constant constellation,
rounded rose of water,
on
poor people's
dining tables.

Generously
you give up
your balloon of freshness
to the boiling consummation
of the pot,
and in the blazing heat of the oil
the shred of crystal
is transformed into a curled feather
    of gold.

I shall also proclaim how your
influence livens the salad's love,
and the sky seems to contribute
giving you the fine shape of hail

y destinada
a relucir,
constelación constante,
redonda rosa de agua,
sobre
la mesa
de las pobres gentes.

Generosa
deshaces
tu globo de frescura
en la consumación
ferviente de la olla,
y el jirón de cristal
al calor encendido del aceite
se transforma en rizada pluma
    de oro.

También recordaré cómo fecunda
tu influencia el amor de la ensalada
y parece que el cielo contribuye
dándote fina forma de granizo

praising your chopped brightness
upon the halves of the tomato.
But within the people's
reach,
showered with oil,
dusted
with a pinch of salt,
you satisfy the worker's hunger
along the hard road home.
Poor people's star,
fairy godmother
wrapped
in fancy paper,
you rise from the soil,
eternal, intact, as pure
as a celestial seed,
and when the kitchen knife
cuts you
the only painless tear
is shed:
you made us weep without suffering.
I have praised every living thing,
  onion,

a celebrar tu claridad picada
sobre los hemisferios de un tomate.
Pero al alcance
de las manos del pueblo,
regada con aceite,
espolvoreada
con un poco de sal,
matas el hambre
del jornalerno en el duro camino.
Estrella de los pobres,
hada madrina
envuelta
en delicado
papel, sales del suelo,
eterna, intacta, pura
como semilla de astro,
y al cortarte
el cuchillo en la cocina
sube la única lágrima
sin pena.
Nos hiciste llorar sin afligirnos.
Yo cuanto existe celebré,
  cebolla,

but for me you are
more beautiful than a bird
of blinding plumage;
to my eyes you are
a heavenly balloon, platinum cup,
the snowy anemone's
motionless dance.

The fragrance of earth is alive
in your crystalline nature.

pero para mí eres
más hermosa que un ave
de plumas cegadoras,
eres para mis ojos
globo celeste, copa de platino,
baile inmóvil
de anémona nevada

y vive la fragancia de la tierra
en tu naturaleza cristalina.

Pablo Neruda
translation by Ken Krabbenhoft

The Traveling Onion

*It is believed that the onion originally came from India. In Egypt it was
an object of worship—why I haven't been able to find out. From Egypt
the onion entered Greece and on to Italy, thence into all of Europe.*
—Better Living Cookbook

When I think how far the onion has traveled
just to enter my stew today, I could kneel and praise
all small forgotten miracles,
crackly paper peeling on the drainboard,
pearly layers in smooth agreement,
the way knife enters onion
and onion falls apart on the chopping block,
a history revealed.

And I would never scold the onion
for causing tears.
It is right that tears fall
for something small and forgotten.
How at meal, we sit to eat,
commenting on texture of meat or herbal aroma
but never on the translucence of onion,
now limp, now divided,
or its traditionally honorable career:
For the sake of others,
disappear.

Naomi Shihab Nye

The Mind of Squash

*Overnight, and quietly. Beneath the scratchy leaf we thicken
and expand so fast you can't believe. Sun pours into us. We
drink midnight too, blue locust lullaby feeding our graceful
sleep. When you come back, we are fat. Doubled in the dark.
Faster than you are. Sometimes we grow together, two of us
twining out from the same stalk, conversational blossoms. Bring
the bucket. Bring the small knife with the sharp blade. Bring
the wind to cool our wide span of leaves, each one bigger than a
human head, bigger than dinner plates. Wait till you find the
giant prize we have hidden from you all along—no muscle-
rich upper arm exceeds its size. But the farmer doesn't like it.
Too big for selling, he says. Only for zucchini bread. Never
mind. We like it. We have our own pride.*

Naomi Shihab Nye

Perhaps the World Ends Here

The world begins at the kitchen table. No matter what, we must eat to live.

The gifts of earth are brought and prepared, set on the table. So it has been since creation, and it will go on.

We chase chickens or dogs away from it. Babies teethe at the corners. They scrape their knees under it.

It is here that children are given instructions on what it means to be human. We make men at it, we make women.

At this table we gossip, recall enemies and the ghosts of lovers.

Our dreams drink coffee with us as they put their arms around our children. They laugh with us at our poor falling-down selves and as we put ourselves back together once again at the table.

This table has a house in the rain, an umbrella in the sun.

Wars have begun and ended at this table. It is a place to hide in the shadow of terror. A place to celebrate the terrible victory.

We have given birth on this table, and prepared our parents for burial here.

At this table we sing with joy, with sorrow. We pray of suffering and remorse. We give thanks.

Perhaps the world will end at the kitchen table, while we are laughing and crying, eating of the last sweet bite.

Joy Harjo

For the Love of Earth

I will wade out
      till my thighs are steeped in burning flowers
i will take the sun in my mouth
and leap into the ripe air
        Alive

E. E. Cummings

A Blessing

I ask all blessings,
I ask them with reverence,
of my mother the earth,
of the sky, moon, and sun my father.
I am old age: the essence of life,
I am the source of all happiness.
All is peaceful, all in beauty,
all in harmony, all in joy.

Source unknown

Corn Mother

When Kloskurbeh, the All-maker, lived on earth, there were no people yet. But one day when the sun was high, a youth appeared and called him "Uncle, brother of my mother." This young man was born from the foam of the waves, foam quickened by the wind and warmed by the sun. It was the motion of the wind, the moistness of water, and the sun's warmth which gave him life—-warmth above all, because warmth is life. And the young man lived with Kloskurbeh and became his chief helper.

Now, after these two powerful beings had created all manner of things, there came to them, as the sun was shining at high noon, a beautiful girl. She was born of the wonderful earth plant, and of the dew, and of warmth. Because a drop of dew fell on a leaf and was warmed by the sun, and the warming sun is life, this girl came into being—from the green living plant, from moisture, and from warmth.

"I am love," said the maiden. "I am a strength giver. I am the nourisher; I am the provider of men and animals. They all love me."

Then Kloskurbeh thanked the Great Mystery Above for having sent them the maiden. The youth, the Great Nephew, married her, and the girl conceived and thus became First Mother. And Kloskurbeh, the Great Uncle, who teaches humans all they need to know, taught their children how to live. Then he went away to dwell in the north, from which he will return sometime when he is needed.

Now the people increased and became numerous. They lived by hunting, and the more people there were, the less game they found. They were hunting it out, and as the animals decreased, starvation came upon the people. And First Mother pitied them.

The little children came to First Mother and said: "We are hungry. Feed us." But she had nothing to give them, and she wept. She told them: "Be patient. I will make some food. Then your little bellies will be full." But she kept weeping.

Her husband asked: "How can I make you smile? How can I make you happy?"

"There is only one thing that will stop my tears."

"What is it?" asked her husband.

"It is this: you must kill me."

"I could never do that."

"You must, or I will go on weeping and grieving forever."

Then the husband traveled far, to the end of the earth, to the north he went, to ask the Great Instructor, his uncle Kloskurbeh, what he should do.

"You should do what she wants. You must kill her," said Kloskurbeh. Then the young man went back to his home, and it was his turn to weep. But First Mother said: "Tomorrow at high noon you must do it. After you have killed me, let two of our sons take hold of my hair and drag my body over that empty patch of earth. Let them drag me back and forth, back and forth, over every part of the patch, until all my flesh has been torn from my body. Afterwards, take my bones, gather them up, and bury them in the middle of this clearing. Then leave that place."

She smiled and said, "Wait seven moons and then come back, and you will find my flesh there, flesh given out of love, and it will nourish and strengthen you forever and ever."

So it was done. The husband slew his wife, and her sons, praying, dragged her body to and fro as she commanded, until her flesh covered all the earth. Then they took up her bones and buried them in the middle of it. Weeping loudly, they went away.

When the husband and his children and his children's children came back to that place after seven moons had passed, they found the earth covered with tall, green, tasseled plants. The plants' fruit—corn—was First Mother's flesh, given so that the people might live and flourish. And they partook of First Mother's flesh and found it sweet beyond words. Following her instructions, they did not eat all, but put many kernels back into the earth. In this way her flesh and spirit renewed themselves every seven months, generation after generation.

And First Mother's husband called the plant *skarmunal*, corn.

"Remember," her husband told the people," and take good care of First Mother's flesh, because it is her goodness become substance. Remember her and think of her whenever you eat. . . because she has given her life so that you might live. Yet she is not dead, she lives: in undying love she renews herself again and again."

Penobscot

Reliefs

The rain, dancing, long-haired,
ankles silvered by lightning,
descends, to an accompaniment of drums:
the corn opens its eyes, and grows.

Relieves

La lluvia, pie danzante y largo pelo,
el tobillo mordido por el rayo,
desciende acompañada de tambores:
abre los ojos el maíz, y crece.

Octavio Paz
translation by Muriel Rukeyser

Grow

Waters of the earth,
bring us new hope for our crops
which will grow like a newborn fawn
shyly taking its first look
at the world around her.

George Clark, 3rd grade

Two Rain Songs (Papago)

1.
Close to the west the great ocean is singing.
The waves are rolling toward me, covered with many clouds.
Even here I catch the sound.
The earth is shaking beneath me and I hear the deep rumbling.

2.
A cloud on top of Evergreen Mountain is singing,
A cloud on top of Evergreen Mountain is standing still,
It is raining and thundering up there,
It is raining here,
Under the mountain the corn tassels are shaking,
Under the mountain the horns of the child corn are glistening.

Winged Serpent

Mother Nature

Mother Nature sighs
as she starts to repair the Year.
The Year has forgotten her coat again
and she is cold and bare.

Mother Nature knits a design
of pink buds and green swirls of mist.
When Mother Nature finishes the last tree,
she weaves in all the wonders of the world.

Little yellow birds flitter under her needle
as Mother Nature adds texture,
then humans,
then love.

Sylvie Krekow, 4th grade

Starting with Little Things

Love the earth like a mole,
fur-near. Nearsighted,
hold close the clods,
their fine-print headlines.
Pat them with soft hands –
Like spades, but pink and loving: they
break rock, nudge giants aside,
affable plow.
Fields are to touch.
each day nuzzle your way.

Tomorrow the world.

William Stafford

An Insider's View of the Garden

How can I help but admire the ever perseverant
unquenchable dill
that sways like an unruly crowd at a soccer match
waving its lacy banners
where garlic belongs or slyly invading a hill
of Delicata squash—
how can I help but admire such ardor? I seek it

as bees the flower's core, hummingbirds
that concocted sugar water
that lures them to the feeder in the lilacs.
I praise the springy mane
of untamed tendrils asprawl on chicken wire
that promise to bring forth
peas to overflow a pillowcase.

Some days I adore my coltish broccolis,
the sketchbook beginnings
of their green heads still encauled, incipient trees
sprung from the Pleistocene.
Some days the leeks, that Buckingham Palace patrol
and the quarter-mile of beans
—green, yellow, soy, lima, bush and pole—

demand applause. As do dilatory parsnips,
a ferny dell of tops
regal as celery. Let me laud onion that erupts
slim as a grass stem
then spends the summer inventing its pungent tulip
and the army of brussel sprouts
extending its spoon-shaped leaves oven dozens of armpits

that conceal what are now merely thoughts, mere nubbins
needing long ripening.
But let me lament my root-maggot-raddled radishes
my bony and bored red peppers
that drop their lower leaves like dancehall strippers
my cauliflowers that spit
out thimblesize heads in the heat and take beetles to bed.

O children, citizens, my wayward jungly dears
you are all to be celebrated
plucked, transplanted, tilled under, resurrected here
—even the lowly despised
purslane, chickweed, burdock, poke, wild poppies.
For all of you, whether eaten or extirpated
I plan to spend the rest of my life on my knees.

Maxine Kumin

Yes

—

i thank You God for most this amazing
day: for the leaping greenly spirits of trees
and a blue true dream of sky; and for everything
which is natural which is infinite which is yes

(i who have died am alive again today,
and this is the sun's birthday; this is the birth
day of life and of love and wings: and of the gay
great happening illimitably earth)

how should tasting touching hearing seeing
breathing any—lifted from the no
of all nothing—human merely being
doubt unimaginable You?
(now the ears of my ears awake and
now the eyes of my eyes are open)

E. E. Cummings

Cuttings

Sticks-in-a-drowse droop over sugary loam,
Their intricate stem-fur dries;
But still the delicate slips keep coaxing up water
The small cells bulge;

One nub of growth
Nudges a sand-crumb loose,
Pokes through a musty sheath
Its pale tendrilous horn.

Cuttings

(later)

This urge, wrestle, resurrection of dry sticks,
Cut stems struggling to put down feet,
What saint strained so much,
Rose on such lopped limbs to a new life?

I can hear, underground, that sucking and sobbing,
In my veins, in my bones I feel it,—
The small waters seeping upward,
The tight grains parting at last.
When sprouts break out,
Slippery as fish,
I quail, lean to beginnings, sheath-wet.

Theodore Roethke

Weaving the Morning

One rooster does not weave a morning,
he will always need the other roosters,
one to pick up the shout and toss it to another,
another rooster to pick up that shout
and toss it to another, and many other roosters
to criss-cross the sun-threads of their rooster-shouts
so that the morning, starting from a frail cobweb,
may go on being woven, among all the roosters.

And growing larger, becoming cloth,
pitching a tent where they all may enter,
unfurling itself for them all, the tent
(the morning) soars free of ties and ropes—
the morning, tent of a weave so light
that, woven, it lifts through itself: balloon light.

João Cabral de Melo Neto
translation by Galway Kinnell

Tecendo a manhã

Um galo sózinho não tece uma manhã:
êle precisará sempre de outros galos.
De um que apanhe êsse grito que êle
e o lance a outro; de um outro galo
que apanhe o grito que um galo antes
e o lance a outro; e de outros galos
que com muitos outros galos se cruzem
os fios de sol de seus gritos de galo,
para que a manhã, desde uma teia tênue,
se vá tecendo, entre todos os galos.

E se encorpando em tela, entre todos,
se erguendo tenda, onde entrem todos,
se entretendendo para todos, no tôldo
(a manhã) que plana livre de armação.
A manhã, tôldo de um tecido tão aéreo
que, tecido, se eleva por si: luz balão.

João Cabral de Melo Neto

O Taste and See

The world is
not with us enough.
O taste and see

the subway Bible poster said,
meaning **The Lord**, meaning
if anything all that lives
to the imagination's tongue,

grief, mercy, language,
tangerine, weather to
breathe them, bite,
savor, chew, swallow, transform

into our flesh our
deaths, crossing the street, plum, quince,
living in the orchard and being

hungry and picking
the fruit.

Denise Levertov

Gathering the Wild Figs—Vizcaina, Gomera

They are plump
and deeply purple.
Hungry and hot
we gorge ourselves
on their rich, red sweetnesses
that break into our mouths
like last and urgent kisses.
They are how this island rewards
our loving her so well
our venturing into the ache
of all her beauty
and abiding the gaze
of her myriad faces
with our myriad faces.
She was broken
but pieced herself together again
from the shards of the lava flow
from the destruction
she grew beautiful and strong.
Today we have paid the price
for her unveiling.
We have seen her scars
and she is not pleased
but ay

how she wanted us to see.
Ay, how we have hungered and thirsted to see.
And here her bounty.
We will taste her wild figs forever.
When we are old
our breaths will be scented with her wildness.
When we die we will know where we go.

Emilia Paredes

To have the whole air!

To have the whole air!
The light, the full sun
Coming down on the flowerheads,
The tendrils turning slowly,
A slow snail-lifting, liquescent;
To be by the rose
Rising slowly out of its bed,
Still as a child in its first loneliness;
To see cyclamen veins become clearer in early sunlight,
And mist lifting out of the brown cattails;
To stare into the after-light, the glitter left on the lake's surface,
When the sun has fallen behind a wooded island;
To follow the drops sliding from a lifted oar,
Held up, while the rower breathes, and the small boat drifts
        quietly shoreward;
To know that light falls and fills, often without our knowing,
As an opaque vase fills to the brim from a quick pouring,
Fills and trembles at the edge yet does not flow over,
Still holding and feeding the stem of the contained flower.

Theodore Roethke

Too lazy to be ambitious

Too lazy to be ambitious,
I let the world take care of itself.
Ten days' worth of rice in my bag;
a bundle of twigs by the fireplace.
Why chatter about delusion and enlightenment?
Listening to the night rain on my roof,
I sit comfortably, with both legs stretched out.

Ryōkan
1758-1831

Earth, isn't this what you want

Earth, isn't this
      what you want:
            rising up
inside us *invisibly*
      once more?
            Isn't it your dream
to be invisible someday?
      Earth! invisible!
            What, is it
you urgently ask for
      if not transformation?
            Earth, my love,
I will do it.
      Believe me,
            your springtimes
are no longer needed
      to win me—*one*
            just one, is already
too much for my blood.
      I have been yours
            unable to say so
from the beginning.

Rainer Maria Rilke
Excerpt from Ninth Elegy
translation by David Young

The Lake Isle of Innisfree

I will arise and go now, and go to Innisfree,
And a small cabin build there, of clay and wattles made:
Nine bean rows will I have there, a hive for the honeybee,
And live alone in the bee-loud glade.

And I shall have some peace there, for peace comes dropping slow,
Dropping from the veils of the morning to where the cricket sings;
There midnight's all a-glimmer, and noon a purple glow,
And evening full of the linnet's wings.

I will arise and go now, for always night and day
I hear lake water lapping with low sounds by the shore;
While I stand on the roadway, or on the pavements grey,
I hear it in the deep heart's core.

William Butler Yeats

The Peace of Wild Things

When despair for the world grows in me
and I wake in the night at the least sound
in fear of what my life and my children's lives may be,
I go and lie down where the wood drake
rests in his beauty on the water, and the great heron feeds.
I come into the peace of wild things
who do not tax their lives with forethought
of grief. I come into the presence of still water.
And I feel above me the day-blind stars
waiting with their light. For a time
I rest in the grace of the world, and am free.

Wendell Berry

Groundhog Day

Celebrate this unlikely oracle,
this ball of fat and fur,
whom we so mysteriously endow
with the power to predict spring.
Let's hear it for the improbable heroes who,
frightened at their own shadows,
nonetheless unwittingly work miracles.
Why shouldn't we believe
this peculiar rodent holds power
over the sun and seasons in his stubby paw?
Who says that God is all grandeur and glory?

Unnoticed in the earth, worms
are busily, brainlessly, tilling the soil.
Field mice, all unthinking, have scattered
seeds that will take root and grow.
Grape hyacinths, against all reason,
have been holding up green shoots beneath the snow.
How do you think that spring arrives?
There is nothing quieter, nothing
more secret, miraculous, mundane.

Do you want to play your part
in bringing it to birth? Nothing simpler.
Find a spot not too far from the ground
and wait.

Lynn Ungar

(O sweet spontaneous)

O sweet spontaneous
earth how often have
the
doting

      fingers of
prurient philosophers pinched
and
poked

thee
, has the naughty thumb
of science prodded
thy

    beauty   . how
often have religions taken
thee upon their scraggy knees
squeezing and

buffeting thee that thou mightest conceive
gods
      (but
true

to the incomparable
couch of death thy
rhythmic
lover

      thou answerest

them only with

           spring)

E. E. Cummings

Spring Song

the green of Jesus

is breaking the ground

and the sweet

smell of delicious Jesus

is opening the house and

the dance of Jesus music

has hold of the air and

the world is turning

in the body of Jesus and

the future is possible

Lucille Clifton

In the Fields

In the fields, trees stand tall and still
like hard rocks.
When the spring comes,
the buds on each flower
shoot out for their first breath.

The air is like mounds of food
coming each millisecond.
The flowers absorb the rain
as if that was how they're made.
Now the buds have bloomed
into the last stage.

Kyle Fukuhara, 3rd grade

Apples

Apples swirl like the wind
blowing strong.
The apples fall from the sky
to make rain.
Apples twirl like the ocean swimming.
Apples dance from the sky
like chipmunks throwing nuts.

Eboné Jones, 2nd grade

Gushing with Color

The flowers glow with color in spring,
so animals can find their way at night.
Flowers in summer gush with color,
so painters don't have to pay for their hues.
In the winter, the flowers are so sad
because they can't show their colors.
In the fall, the flowers see all the leaves,
and they brag how beautiful they are.
The flower's best friend is the warmth,
the only one who sees the roots. Flowers
write letters to their cousins and
grandmothers because they have
feelings, too.

Adrian Rautureau, 2nd grade

Peas Conference

Peas climb vines to a peace
conference to meet the trees.
The trees paint pictures of the vines.
Then the peas
and trees astonish people
with the idea
of peace everywhere
as they grow
peace around the world.

Sam Baird, 2nd grade

A Raindrop

A raindrop spreads his arms
to catch his best friends.

He and his friends land on a dry, dirt road,
and everything around them is dusty and brown.

They go walking hand in hand,
and friendship starts flowing out behind them.

The trails of friendship join
and everything behind them springs to life.

The grass turns green
and even the road gets moist.

Their fat little legs become skinny
because they are turning fit.

His friends find other companions,
and they join hands.

Soon their friendship reaches around the world,
and everyone runs to get their friends
and join the flowing of friendship.

Soon the world is overflowed with friendship,
and everyone goes home
with not one but many friends.

Camilla Gardiner, 3rd grade

Fruit

Fruit brings people food
and keeps them healthy.
Fruit lets you know
that the trees are alive.
Fruit glistens in the air
and silently falls down from the tree fast.
Fruit is as wet and soft
as a chocolate cake.
I think fruit makes animals get healthy.

Alex Raubvogel, 2nd grade

In the winter

In the winter, trees make sap
for my maple syrup.
I can't eat pancakes without it.
The pancakes try to eat the syrup
before I do. They never succeed.
Back to the tree,
people rub it for sap.

Gill Biesold-McGee, 2nd grade

In the spring

In the spring, the moss
wakes up with a yawn
and gets his coffee to perk him up.
Then moss gets ready to make people slip.
His doorbell rings.
Moss opens it, and weeds
spring up from the ground.
"Hello," they say.
The weeds invite themselves
to plant their roots in the moss' house.
The moss says, "Get out of here,"
but at the same moment,
the weeds turn into tulips.

Gill Biesold-McGee, 2nd grade

Remember

Remember the sky you were born under,
know each of the star's stories.
Remember the moon, know who she is.
Remember the sun's birth at dawn, that is the
strongest point of time. Remember sundown
and the giving away to night.
Remember your birth, how your mother struggled
to give you form and breath. You are evidence of
her life, and her mother's, and hers.
Remember your father. He is your life, also.
Remember the earth whose skin you are:
red earth, black earth, yellow earth, white earth,
brown earth, we are earth.
Remember the plants, trees, animal life who all have their
tribes, their families, their histories, too. Talk to them,
listen to them. They are alive poems.
Remember the wind. Remember her voice. She knows the
origin of this universe.
Remember you are all people and all people
are you.

Remember you are this universe and this
universe is you.
Remember all is in motion, is growing, is you.
Remember language comes from this.
Remember the dance language is, that life is.
Remember.

Joy Harjo

Author Index

First Line Index

First Line Index

Arnold, Bob, "No Tool or Rope or Pail." Reprinted from WHERE RIVERS MEET, Mad River Press, 1990. Permission sought.*

Berry, Wendell, "Manifesto," "The Peace of Wild Things," and "The Man Born to Farming." Reprinted from THE SELECTED POEMS OF WENDELL BERRY, Counterpoint Press, 1998. Permission requested.

Budbill, David, "The First Green of Spring," from MOMENT TO MOMENT: POEMS OF A MOUNTAIN RECLUSE, Copyright © 1999 by David Budbill. Reprinted by permission of Copper Canyon Press.

Cabral de Melo Neto, João, "Weaving the Morning," from AN ANTHOLOGY OF TWENTIETH-CENTURY BRAZILIAN POETRY, edited by Elizabeth Bishop and Emanuel Brasil, copyright © 1972 Wesleyan University Press. Permission requested.

Clifton, Lucille, "cutting greens" and "Spring Song," copyright 1987 by Lucille Clifton. Reprinted from GOOD WOMAN: POEMS AND A MEMOIR 1969–1980, with the permission of BOA Editions, Ltd.

Cummings, E. E., "(O sweet spontaneous)" and "Yes," from E. E. CUMMINGS, SELECTED POEMS, edited by Richard S. Kennedy, Liveright Publishing, 1994. Permission requested.

Fallon, Peter, "The Meadow," from THE NEWS AND WEATHER, Gallery Press, Dublin, 1987. Permission requested.

Flanders, Jane, "Dandelion Greens," by Jane Flanders. First appeared in the Quarterly Review of Literature's Poetry Book Series title: LEAVING AND COMING BACK. Permission sought.*

Garza, Eliza, "Why I Make the Best Barrels," from Verse, Vol. II, No. 1, 1994. Permission sought.*

Gaspar de Alba, Alicia, "Making Tortillas," by Alicia Gaspar de Alba. Reprinted from THREE TIMES A WOMAN: CHICANA POETRY (1989) with permission of Bilingual Press/Editorial Bilingue, Arizona State University.

Grace, Patricia, "Butterflies" by Patricia Grace. Reprinted from ELECTRIC CITY AND OTHER STORIES (1987) Penguin, New Zealand. Reprinted by permission of Penguin Books, New Zealand.

Gruchow, Paul, "The Transfiguration of Bread," by Paul Gruchow, from GRASS ROOTS: THE UNIVERSE OF HOME, 1988, Milkweed Editions, 1988. Permission requested.

Hall, Donald, "Names of Horses" and "Ox Cart Man," by Donald Hall. Reprinted from OLD AND NEW POEMS: DONALD HALL, Houghton Mifflin, 1990. Permission requested.

Harjo, Joy, "Remember," from SHE HAD SOME HORSES by Joy Harjo. Copyright © 1983 by Thunder's Mouth Press. Reprinted by permission of Thunder's Mouth Press. "Perhaps the World Ends Here," from THE WOMAN WHO FELL FROM THE SKY, copyright © 1994, W. W. Norton. Permission requested.

Heaney, Seamus, "Follower," by Seamus Heaney, from NORTH, Faber & Faber, 1975. "The Seed Cutters," by Seamus Heaney, from DEATH OF A NATURALIST, Faber & Faber, 1969. Permission requested.

Hennen, Tom, "Soaking Up the Sun," by Tom Hennen, from CRAWLING OUT THE WINDOW, Black Hat Press, 1998. Permission sought.*

Hogan, Linda, "Potatoes," by Linda Hogan, from SEEING THROUGH THE SUN, copyright © 1985 by Linda Hogan. Reprinted by permission of University of Massachusetts Press.

Hughes, Langston, "Dream Dust," by Langston Hughes, from MONTAGE OF A DREAM DEFERRED, Holt, 1951; copyright © estate of Langston Hughes. Permission sought.*

Permissions & Copyrights

Kavanaugh, Patrick, excerpt from "Tarry Flynn," by Patrick Kavanaugh from PATRICK KAVANAUGH, THE COLLECTED POEMS, Devin-Adair Publishers, Inc., 1973. Used by permission of the publisher.

Kids Write for the Earth, "Peas Conference," by Sam Baird; "In the Spring" and "In the Winter," by Gill Biesold-McGee; "Grow," by George Clark; "In the Fields," by Kyle Fukuhara; "A Raindrop," by Camilla Gardiner; "Worms of Mystery," by Elise Greiner; "Apples," by Eboné Jones; "Mother Nature," by Sylvie Krekow; "A Recipe for a Garden," by Henry Phillips; "Fruit," by Alex Raubvogel; "Gushing with Color," by Adrian Rautureau; "Bees," by Dean Shumway; "Worms," by LaDonna Wilson. All poems used by permission of teacher Shelley Tucker.

Kinsley, Robert, "Those Mornings", copyright © Robert Kinsley reprinted from FIELD STONES, Orchises Press. Reprinted by permission of the author and Orchises Press.

Kirshenmann, Fred, "Rice Lesson," excerpt from "On Becoming Lovers of the Soil," from FOR ALL GENERATIONS: MAKING WORLD AGRICULTURE MORE SUSTAINABLE, OM Publishing, 1997. Permission requested.

Kort, Ellen, "The Gardener" and "Letter from McCarty's Farm," by Ellen Kort. From LETTER FROM McCARTY'S FARM (1994), copyright © 1994, Fox Print, Inc. Permission requested.

Kumar, Amitava, "Primary Lessons in Political Economy," by Amitava Kumar. From THE KAYA ANTHOLOGY OF NEW ASIAN NORTH AMERICAN POETRY (1995). Reprinted by permission of the author.

Kumin, Maxine, "Chores" and "An Insider's View of the Garden," by Maxine Kumin, from CONNECTING THE DOTS (1996), W. W. Norton. Permission requested.

Lee, Li-Young, "From Blossoms," from ROSE, copyright © 1986 by Li-Young Lee. Reprinted with the permission of BOA Editions, Ltd.

Levertov, Denise, "O Taste and See," from POEMS 1960–1967, copyright © 1964 by Denise Levertov. Reprinted by permission of New Directions Publishing Corp.

McPherson, Sandra, excerpt from "Three from the Market," copyright © Sandra McPherson (1973, 2003) from RADIATION (Ecco, 1973). Used by permission of the author.

Michaels, Denise Calvetti, "Returning from Italy," copyright © by Denise Calvetti Michaels. Used by permission of the author.

Nabhan, Gary, "You Make the Earth Good by Your Work," excerpt from THE DESERT SMELLS LIKE RAIN: A NATURALIST IN PAPAGO INDIAN COUNTRY, by Gary P. Nabhan, North Point Press, 1982. Permission requested.

Neruda, Pablo, "Ode to the Apple" and "Ode to the Onion," from ODES TO COMMON THINGS, by Pablo Neruda. Copyright © 1994 by Pablo Neruda and Fundacion Pablo Neruda (Odes Spanish); copyright © 1994 by Ken Krabbenhoft (Odes English Translation); copyright © 1994 by Ferris Cook (Illustrations and Compilation). By permission of Little, Brown and Company, Inc.

Nye, Naomi Shihab, "The Mind of Squash," copyright © Naomi Shihab Nye. Reprinted from MINT SNOWBALL, Anhinga Press. Used by permission of the author and Anhinga Press. "My Father and the Fig Tree" and "The Traveling Onion," copyright © Naomi Shihab Nye. Reprinted from WORDS UNDER THE WORDS, SELECTED POEMS, © 1995, Far Corner Books. Used by permission of the author and Far Corner Books.

O'Reilley, Mary Rose, "Surrender," from THE BARN AT THE END OF THE WORLD: THE APPRENTICESHIP OF A QUAKER BUDDHIST SHEPHERD, by Mary Rose O'Reilley, Milkweed Editions, © 2001. Permission requested.

Colophon

Cover title type is set in Mona Lisa Recut, a typeface redrawn by
A. Pat Hickson in 1991, based on originals created by Albert Auspurg
in 1910. The subtitle type is Interstate. This type is based on the lettering
used on signs of the United States Federal Highway Administration,
designed in 1993 by Tobias Frere-Jones.

Cover stock is 10 point coated one side with matt lamination. Interior stock is
45# Natural.

Cover photographs were gleaned from a variety of copyright-free image banks.
Back cover illustration is the Vincent van Gogh Charcoal sketch *L'émondage
des échalas* from 1888.

Title heads are set in Carlton. This elegant typeface was originally designed in
the early 1900s for the Stephenson Blake Typefoundry. The designers were F.
H. Ehmcke and Esselte Letraset Ltd.

Text blocks were set in AGaramond from Adobe Type. AGaramond is a
recasting of the classic serif type face Garamond, originally designed in the
16th century by Claude Garamond. The new Adobe AGaramond was
designed by Robert Slimbach in 1989.

Section page images were selected from copyright-free image banks.

Book design by Tracy Lamb, Jackson Hole, Wyoming.

Print production by Central Plains Book Mfg., Winfield, Kansas.

About the Editor

Claudia Mauro is the founding director of Whit Press—a Seattle-based, nonprofit literary arts organization. Whit Press's mission is to nurture and promote literary work from women writers, writers from ethnic and social minorities, young writers, and first-time authors.

Mauro is the recipient of a Seattle Arts Commission Award, a Hedgebrook Fellowship, Whiteley Center Fellowship, and Jack Straw Writers Fellowship. She was a selected poet for King County's *Poetry on the Buses* project. She has published two collections of poetry, *Stealing Fire* (Whiteaker, 1996) and *Reading the River* (Whiteaker, 1999). Her work appears in various journals throughout the Northwest. She lives and writes in Seattle, Washington.

About Whit Press

The truth of our lives—the power of our stories.
Support for the Independent Voice.

Our Mission:

Whit Press is a Seattle-based, nonprofit publishing organization dedicated to the transformational power of the written word.

We create books that use literature as a tool in support of other nonprofit organizations working toward environmental and social justice.

Whit Press also exists as an oasis to nurture and promote the rich diversity of literary work from women writers, writers from ethnic and social minorities, young writers, and first-time authors.

We are dedicated to producing beautiful books that combine outstanding literary content with design excellence.

Whit Press brings you the best of fiction, creative nonfiction, and poetry from diverse literary voices who do not have easy access to quality publication.

We publish stories of creative discovery, cultural insight, human experience, spiritual exploration, and more.

Whit Press, Inc.
Richard Hugo House
1634 Eleventh Avenue
Seattle, WA 98122
whitpress@aol.com